Smiling Angels Two

By
Suzanne Jennifer Morton

First Published and Printed in February 2009
by Suzanne Jennifer Morton

ISBN: 978 0 9556020 1 6

Printed by: R. Booth Ltd, The Praze, Penryn, Cornwall
Tel: 01326 373628   www.rboothltd.co.uk

Acknowledgements

I dedicate this book to the many readers who read and enjoyed 'Smiling Angels' and wanted me to write another book. Thank you for the confidence you have given me to move forward with my writing. I am especially grateful to everyone who has supported me, and helped to make it a success. THANK YOU ALL.

Introduction

I have been pleasantly surprised and amazed by the success of my first book 'Smiling Angels', which I wrote and published in 2007. The volume of sales led to a reprint in 2008, and I have received hundreds of letters from readers saying how they couldn't put it down until they had finished it, and how inspirational it was. I have had many requests to write another book, and this, together with the continued success of 'Smiling Angels' has given me the encouragement and confidence to write 'Smiling Angels Two'.

This second book is my very frank and personal account of memorable moments throughout my life, of angel encounters and experiences. I hope you will find it both moving and inspirational.

Chapter 1

Sitting here yet again on East Looe sea front, it's hard to imagine a more beautiful sight, rain or shine. Night times are just as spectacular, with the lights from hotels, guest houses and cottages built high into the hillsides towering above bringing the river to life with their reflections. Yes, we've been on foreign holidays, seen white sands, clear blue skies and palm trees, but for me nothing compares with the magic of this heavenly place, a place I know I have lived before in another life. Looking out to sea, there are usually Naval Ships, large ferries or ocean liners to be seen on the horizon, beautiful yachts and fishing boats bobbing up and down whilst seagulls hover above in anticipation of a good feed. Sometimes I have to pinch myself in case it's all just a lovely dream that I live here with my kind and loving husband James, our adorable black and white cat Charlie and my two beautiful daughters Tracy and Michelle, my handsome grandson Robert, and also Michelle and Chris's gorgeous baby daughter Keira Grace, who was born on February 1st 2008 all living close by. Tracy, her husband and Robert moved here about three years ago. It was definitely a move that was meant to be for Robert, and I believe the move and his Angels helped to save his life. I will tell you that moving story later on, as I want to share with you just a few memorable moments I have had in my life.

I was born in a private nursing home in Ashbourne, Derbyshire in May 1947, and my mum was living with my gran and grandpa in their grand imposing house in Matlock. They were quite wealthy at the time and had a maid and nanny, although mum insisted on spending most of her time with me, and wouldn't let the nanny take me out for walks as she used to love taking me to Matlock Park just down the hill from where we lived. She had her favourite seat opposite the boating lake, and would sit for hours feeding the ducks and chatting to people. With her natural blonde hair and blue eyes, mum was stunningly beautiful and had the same slim elegant figure as her mum. Yes, gran was slim, elegant and every inch a lady, her whole being just oozed grandness. I have no memories of grandpa at all as he died when I was a little girl.

My dad was in the army at the time of my birth and based in Egypt, so he never got to see me until I was nearly one year old. It wasn't long after his return that we went to live with his parents in Pleasley, Nottinghamshire, where my sister Angela was born when I was two years old. Dad was tall, dark and handsome and he and mum made an attractive couple. I don't think mum liked living with grandma and grandad very much because mum wanted me to talk nicely and grandma used to come out with quite a lot of slang words, which mum hated.

We lived in the old part of Pleasley near the colliery where my grandad worked as a winder. There were several rows of old terraced houses where we lived, but as I recall from my many happy memories of school holidays spent with my devoted grandparents, all the windows would sparkle in the sunlight all along the street, and early in the mornings you could often see the women of the house scrubbing their front steps with their scarf tied in a turban to cover hair curlers, which in those days looked like silver coloured metal clips. With the outside toilet and tin bath in front of the fire, it must have been quite a reality check for mum as she had been used to more grander surroundings. Grandma was quite well built and was a fantastic cook, even though she cooked on the fire and baked bread in the coal oven. Grandad had the most amazing blue eyes, I remember, and I don't recall a time when he didn't have a shirt and tie on, even when he was gardening. He was a true gentleman and would take me out on long country walks as I got older and went to stay in the school holidays. Grandma used to take me to chapel on Sundays and seemed to have an endless supply of hats for all occasions. She had the kindest face you could imagine, and taught me to knit and sew as we listened to the radio, as it was quite a while before they could afford a television.

When I was three and a half years old, we went to live in Clipstone, Nottinghamshire, a mainly mining village and my brother Ron was born soon after, so my mum had her hands full as you can imagine. My dad worked at the colliery there and went to college in Mansfield most weekday evenings, where he started his run up the ladder to become a colliery manager.

My first ever memory was when I was three and a half years old. We lived on Sixth Avenue in Clipstone in a small house. There were terraced houses in blocks of three with smallish front and massive back gardens. A few doors up the street from us, a dark haired boy called Paul, an only child, lived with his parents and their black Scotty dog called Jingy. I remember being terrified of the dog, because it used to bark loudly whenever I used to call for Paul to ask if he was coming out to play. Their house looked exactly the same as ours from the outside, but inside

I remember it being quite posh compared with ours, not that ours was a mess or anything but it just seemed posher. In those days you didn't need to watch your children as much as you do nowadays and although we were only three, we were allowed to go down a little path and on to some wasteland that used to be called The Bay. There were mountains of gardening rubbish that people used to dump, but it still looked quite nice to me with pretty flowers popping up here and there on top of the mounds. Paul and I sat on the ground picking buttercups and daisies to take home for our mums, and then he showed me a new shiny coin. I was fascinated with this coin as I had never seen one before, so he said that he would give it to me to keep if I showed him my bottom. We didn't know at that stage we were being very naughty as I quickly did a moony, as they say. I only realised that I had done wrong after returning home, when dad asked where I had got the money from. I proudly told him that I had only had to show Paul my bottom to get it. I received my first smack that day and was briskly marched off to bed to reflect on my naughtiness, although I didn't think it was fair at the time because no one had told me before that it was wrong to do it. I'm sure Paul got into trouble too.

Over the years my dad was extremely strict with us, especially with me for some reason, and although mum was kind and loving to us, I didn't really enjoy my childhood very much mainly because of dads strict rules. If we spoke at the table during meal times, we had to stand in a corner with our hands on our heads and if we dared to laugh whilst having our meal, then we had to go to bed without any food. I did get pleasure from going to stay with my grandma and grandad in Pleasley though and felt that they were my salvation. In our younger days we didn't have bikes and expensive toys, but I can remember all the children in our street playing happily together with just simple things to do like skipping and hopscotch. We loved playing whip and top, and we would put different coloured chalk round the tops so that when we whipped them it looked really pretty when they spun around.

I was eleven years old when I had my first angel experience and during that year I had three accidents, all in the same pink and white striped dress too! By that age, my long dark pigtails had been cut off at Barks hairdressers in Mansfield, and I was transformed into a sophisticated young lady, well on the outside anyway, but underneath it all I was still a bit of a tomboy. One summers day, my nine year old sister Angela who was also dressed in pink and sporting blonde pigtails, together with two of her friends and three of mine, all decided to walk the half mile or so to what was called Vicars Pond. This area was behind the village shops and after just a short walk over wasteland where masses of pretty lilac heather grew wild, we eventually came to the pit tips. These were mountains of varying sizes made up of cobbles and coal dust, with gorse bushes growing down both sides, and to the back of them was the green, slimy water of Vicars Pond below. As we walked along the footpath next to the pond, we decided to be brave and climb the first pit tip, which just happened to be the largest. It didn't help with us all wearing strappy sandals as we huffed and puffed our way to the top. Once there, a sense of achievement came over me as I admired the views of the village shops, village hall and then the park beyond, with the Methodist Chapel to one side of it and the Church of England the other. We were all pushing and shoving each other in order to be the first one to the top of our first conquered mountain, when all of a sudden I remember feeling the cobbles and coal dust beneath my feet moving quite quickly as I struggled to get my grip, and then everything went black.

I was told by my friends afterwards that they watched me roll and bump my way down to the bottom after ripping my way through several gorse bushes, and coming to a stop on the small footpath just short of the slimy pond below. They apparently thought that I was pretending to be dead as they tickled me several times in order to get a response, but to no avail. They shouted a man walking his golden retriever dog and he quickly carried me to his bungalow, with my friends and sister tagging on behind. Apparently I was sick on his lounge carpet as he shouted to one of my friends to run to the doctors surgery to ask them to ring for an ambulance, as in those days you needed to be very rich to afford a home telephone. I think it was about ten days or so that I was in a coma, but I didn't know a thing until I heard laughing and giggling noises, and there before my eyes were cherubs clothed in pale pink dresses running and chasing each other in a misty dell setting near some trees and green still water, with lots of white water lillies floating on the top. The cherubs smiled at me, and then appeared to be rising from the ground one by one as they jumped on to what looked like a Ferris wheel turning very slowly. As it picked up speed, it just looked like a pretty pink Ferris wheel going round and round. I can remember being mesmerised by this sight and hoping that it would slow down so that the cherubs could return to me, but when it eventually did slow down, the pink turned to white, and when it stopped a tall white angel emerged smiling and holding out her hand for me. She was stunningly beautiful, and had the most amazing blue eyes. As I held her hand, we started going round and round on the Ferris wheel, and the next thing I knew I was looking at this beautiful white angel in front of me as she smiled and then disappeared. As I started to come out of my coma and focus on things in the hospital ward, I saw mum and dad sitting by my bed, and when I could manage to talk, I tried to tell them about the cherubs and the white angel going round on the Ferris wheel, but they said it must have been the fan on the table over my bed that I had seen as I had regained consciousness. I know and still do believe that my smiling angels brought me back, my lovely smiling angels.

I will tell you later on about seeing a very special smiling angel when I was in my forties; this was my guardian angel.

Chapter 2

My mum threw the pink and white dress away when I came out of hospital, as I had previously had two more accidents in the same dress, and all were when I was eleven years old.

The first accident was also at Vicars Pond. Mum had sent me to get my brother Ron because he had been gone for most of the day and she was worried about him. I went round the back of the pit tips, along the footpath by the pond, but still saw no sign of him. As

I made my way over a small rackety bridge, I could see the slimy water through the gaps where whole planks of wood had just rotted away, and I had to tread carefully because I was only wearing sandals. My face lit up when I spotted an older boy called Alan who lived not far from us, and, after blushing and feeling butterflies in my stomach, I knew I was having my first crush. Our neighbour Paul was there with my brother, they were just stood over Alan watching him fishing. Paul was quite tall by now, and his dark curly hair hung down over his eyes. My brother Ron looked like a little rascal in his blue shorts and sun hat covering his short blonde hair. He was nearly eight, and mum had her hands full with him because he was always going off on one adventure or another. Forgetting that I was on a mission to bring him home, I listened in awe to Alan's soft voice, and was admiring his shoulder length curly blonde hair whilst he gave us all a fishing lesson. As Alan went to pick up his fishing basket, I asked if he wanted me to hold it for him because he had loads to carry. When he put it over my shoulder, I tried not to show the pain on my face as I struggled with the weight of it. Mum had come to see where we were, and was shouting quite crossly from the other end of the bridge because it was getting quite late by this time. I tried to hurry up, but only got a few feet over the bridge when my foot slipped down a gap, and with the weight of the fishing basket on my shoulder, I almost toppled over and into the water. Alan was behind and recovered his fishing basket, and helped me to my feet before carrying on to the other side. My right leg was starting to bleed, and felt really painful and sore as I limped along the bridge. Ron and Paul were stood next to mum as she shouted again to hurry up. I shouted back that I had hurt my leg and she shouted "Hurry up, it's only a scratch". When I did reach mum she nearly fainted when she saw my leg. I had ripped my right leg open, and the gash was so bad you could see my bone when you mopped the blood up, which was just pumping out. Paul and Alan ran to the doctors surgery to ask them to phone for an ambulance, and it seemed ages before it came, as mum tried to use anything to mop the blood up quickly. She looked quite tired and pale, although she still managed to look beautiful and elegant in her blue sundress and lovely blonde hair.

By this time I was in agony, and starting to feel really weak. Mum had said that she didn't know how the ambulance men were going to reach us with the pit tips being there, and then, all of a sudden, two men in uniforms came running down a smaller pit tip, both holding on to a stretcher. I must say that it looked quite funny to be honest, like something out of a Carry On film. Well, then mum, my brother and I were driven in the ambulance to our house on Sixth Avenue where mum quickly spoke to my dad, who had by this time returned from work to an empty house because my sister had been left with Alan's mum. It was dad who came with me to the hospital, with blue lights flashing and sirens blaring whilst they hurried to get me to Mansfield General Hospital as soon as possible. Dad had changed into grey trousers and a smart navy blazer, and looked handsome with his dark hair and slim build. He waited in the waiting room whilst the nurses wheeled me into a room that smelt of Dettol, and my eyes nearly popped out of my head when I caught sight of the shiny instruments on the trolley now being pushed towards me. I can remember shouting out in pain, well, it was more like screaming actually, as the doctor gave me five injections to numb the pain. It had felt like the needles had been injected into my bone as I cried my eyes out, but the doctor and nurses calmed me down, and told me that if I was really good I could watch whilst they stitched my leg up because I wouldn't feel any more pain. Bandaged from knee to ankle, I was taken to my dad and then driven back home by ambulance. On the way, I proudly told my dad that I had fourteen stitches in my leg, but he didn't believe me because he said he had only heard me shouting out five times, so I must have only had five stitches.

The next day, whilst I was made to rest with my leg raised on a stool, my neighbour Alan and my brother Ron went back to the bridge, to the spot where I had slipped, and they found a six inch rusty nail sticking out that had ripped my leg open and yes, I had been given fourteen stitches in all. I still have the scar to this day, although it's very faded now. I was offered a skin graft later, but when I found out that they had to take some skin from my bum to do it, I'm afraid I just couldn't go through with it. Oh, and in the same pink and white striped dress, after the leg incident, I broke my left arm whilst jiving at the village Youth Club with my friend Sheila. We had been fooling around and I had fallen awkwardly on my arm. Dad asked my Uncle Gordon to come and take a look at it and he put it in a sling, said he didn't think I had broken it, but suggested taking me to the doctors the next day just to be sure. I was in agony all night and didn't sleep a wink. The next day off I went to see the doctor yet again with my mum and we were sent straight to the hospital to have an x-ray, where we discovered I had broken my arm. I can remember getting away with writing at school because my arm was in plaster, until the German teacher threw a piece of chalk at me when he realised I was right handed and it was my left arm I had broken! Oh well, it was good whilst it lasted anyway.

As I said before, dad was extremely strict with us when we were young. I remember that my sister and I had been playing hopscotch just up the road with some other children. My dad asked me a question when we got in, and I said one thing and my sister said the opposite. Once again, as we had experienced many times before, we were made to stand in front of him with our hands on our heads, whilst he sat in an armchair reading his newspaper, and every now and then he would lower it, and with his glasses perched on the end of his nose he looked quite ridiculous as he said "Yes, when you are both ready to tell me which one of you is lying and which one is telling the truth just let me know", and then the newspaper would go up again and every minute seemed like an hour to us. I knew I was telling the truth, so all I could do was protest my innocence, but the time ticked by until we must have been standing in front of him for at least a couple of hours. I stood there thinking how stupid it was and started to laugh, so dad thought that I was the one who was lying and grabbed hold of me, laid me across the dining table and thrashed me with his bare hand on my bottom fourteen times. I know it was fourteen because I counted every agonising whack. When he had finished with me he told me to go to bed. I can't remember how old I was, maybe twelve I think. As I passed my sister, she smirked at me and I felt like knocking her spiteful head off. I was in so much pain I could only lie on my stomach, and as I buried my head in my pillow sobbing uncontrollably, the injustice of being humiliated like that for something I hadn't even done was just too much for me to bear. As I was sobbing, the white angel I had seen whilst I was unconscious just appeared through my pillow, and as her warm smile enveloped me with her love, a calmness came over me and I fell asleep. I had to have a week off school because I couldn't sit down, and my mum wanted to take me to the doctors, but dad said no. Mum was so cross with him, and I remember there being an uncomfortable silence in the house for a few days after that.

Chapter 3

When I was thirteen, my mum was surprised to find out that she was having another baby, and my sister and I were thrilled to bits about the happy news. Mum had the baby at home and I remember her crying and shouting with pain whilst I was in bed one evening. I shared a room with my sister at the time and dad came into us and told us to go back to sleep and that mum was having the baby. I remember it going on for what seemed like a lifetime, all the shouting and screaming, and I put my pillow over my ears to muffle the sound, as I couldn't bear for mum to be suffering. Then it went quiet for a bit before mum started shouting "I don't want it, take it away". At that point, panic and disbelief washed over me. I thought how could she not want her baby, and I started crying for about an hour until dad brought the little baby boy into us and said "Meet your brother David". Mum had been saying that she didn't want gas and air, and for the midwife to take it away! In those days mum and dad did a lot of socialising as dad got one promotion after another, and I remember looking after my baby brother when I came out of school and at weekends, and I was always happy to baby sit when they went out to dinner dances. Mum and dad always looked like film stars; dad with his black dinner jacket and bow-tie, and mum with her long sparkly dresses.

Just after David was born, I went for a walk with my friend and her boyfriend, as I often did when they asked me to. We used to walk to the golf course which was past the pit tips and Vicars Pond, and then up a slight hill and through some woods. We loved it up there as it was so peaceful, and we used to chat for hours eating cherry lips, black jacks and fruit salads. My friend Sheila and her boyfriend started kissing as we lay on the grass in the woods, so I told them I was going for a short walk and would be back soon.

After walking a few hundred yards or so, I bumped into a group of boys from my class at school, there were about ten in all I think. We were all chatting for a few minutes, and as I was passing my bag of black jacks round, a mower started up on the golf course just yards away through the trees, and the aroma of freshly cut grass filled my nostrils. It was a lovely summer evening and I remember feeling really happy at the time, then one boy shouted "Let's give her an examination" and before I could draw breath, I was forced to the ground with them pinning me down and pulling at my blouse until my buttons came undone, and they took it in turns to feel my boobs. One had his hand over my mouth so that I couldn't scream and, just as another of them was trying to remove my pants, I became frantic and struggled so hard that the one with his hand over my mouth got a nasty shock when

I bit him really hard and almost drew blood. At that point I screamed "Get off me you bloody animals" so loud that I think they were afraid someone may have heard me and they all ran off laughing. I was shaking when I got back to my friend Sheila and her boyfriend and they couldn't believe what had happened to me. I was really angry about it when I pulled myself together, and I thought of telling the boys parents about the disturbing incident, but then decided against it. I blamed myself in a way for putting myself in a vulnerable position by walking in the woods alone. I never spoke of it again, well, not until now that is, but even though nearly fifty years have passed since then, I am reminded of it every time I smell freshly cut grass or hear a lawn mower. That was the last time I ever went to Vicars Pond, because something bad always seemed to be waiting for me there. Oh, I tell a lie, I did go back just once more, when I was in my forties. I was staying in Nottingham for Christmas with my brother Ron, his wife Mylena and my niece Bessie, and on Boxing Day he said that he was taking me for a drive and we ended up in a car park near Vicars Pond in Clipstone. I told him that I didn't want to get out of the car but he told me he wanted to show me what had been done to the area since we were children. I only walked a few yards, took one look at the pit tips and the green slimy waters of Vicars Pond and then told him I had to go back to the car as I felt evil spirits all around me. It's not a good place for me to be in, and I will never ever go there again.

A few months later we moved about twenty miles away to a small village called Kirton, just outside Ollerton, because my dad had got another promotion. I was devastated because I had to leave Garibaldi secondary school. It had been a brand new school when my class mates and I had moved to it when we were eleven years old, and I had big plans to stay on for the nursing course that was on offer there when I was old enough. On the day we moved from our terraced house in Clipstone, I cried my eyes out saying goodbye to all my friends and even thought about running away on the day. When we arrived at the house in Kirton, I just couldn't believe my eyes at the sheer size of it. It was a very old house with five bedrooms, a large marble tiled hallway with high ceilings, a massive kitchen with a huge pantry with meat safes on the walls and large hooks hanging everywhere. The two large reception rooms had massive bay windows which overlooked open fields, and to the side of the house there was a large paddock. The back lawn had a small gate at the top with pink roses round the archway leading to an orchard so big it had at least a hundred apple trees, pear trees, plum trees and cherry trees too, with numerous gooseberry, blackberry and raspberry bushes as well as strawberries growing wild and much more. The large wide driveway could have taken at least ten cars with a double garage at the top of it. The front lawn was quite big too with pretty flowers and shrubs everywhere, and the good news for dad was that we had a gardener too! I loved the house, but was mortified that I had to change schools to Winney Lane in Ollerton. My sister, being the rebellious one, got straight on a bus and went to her friends house in Clipstone and said that she wasn't coming home because she didn't want to change schools. In the end dad allowed her and Ron to travel everyday to their old school, but said that because I was nearly fourteen I would be leaving school soon, so I had to stay at Winney Lane school. I hated it with a vengeance, and would cry myself to sleep every night. To make matters worse I needed a new coat, and dad said that he had seen one advertised in the local newspaper and told me it had never been worn. I had loved wearing my navy blue uniform at Garibaldi school, with my smart navy blazer and red and navy striped tie, and had worn it with pride, but when dad gave me this new coat, well, I could cry just telling you about it. To start with, it was bottle green and I had always hated that colour, yes, this green coat complete with hood was a beauty. The sleeves were too long and the length, well, it was nearly to my ankles, this I might add was when mini skirts were in fashion. I used to wear the coat until I was out of sight of the house, then take it off and carry it, even when it was raining or snowing. To top it all, I was bought what dad called sensible shoes, when everyone else in my class wore thin soled fashion shoes. I'll never forget until the day I die the embarrassment I felt, but at least I made some good friends there. Kath and Rosemary were small, pretty and petite whilst Jean was very tall with glasses and I remember her dad being a sergeant in the Police Force, and they lived in a flat over the Police Station. All three of them had hearts of gold, especially Kath who decided to take me under her wing and look out for me. On one occasion I had been suffering from a really bad sore throat, and had called at the tuck shop, a small cabin next door to the school, that morning and bought some sweets called Throaties, I think they were called, to soothe it a bit. I was sitting next to Kath at the time and kept popping these red sugary sweets into my mouth until they had nearly all gone. The next thing I knew, Kath was shaking me because I had slumped forward and gone to sleep on the desk. The teacher told Kath to take me outside to get some fresh air, it was whilst we were outside that she decided to read what was on the packet of sweets only to discover that you could only have two every four hours, and no more than eight a day or something like that. In the end I think I had to be taken home, but I still laugh when I think of that day and of how Kath looked after me so well. We even stayed friends when we both moved to the same town by coincidence about fifteen miles from Ollerton when we were both married. Kath is still married to the same lovely man, and we still send Christmas cards and the occasional letter to each other. I on the other hand went on to have a hell of a time with my first husband.

Chapter 4

I had been smitten with a boy called Alan when I was sixteen (not the fishing Alan from Clipstone). We both worked at Woolworths in Mansfield, where I worked on the ice-cream counter and he in the stock room. Yes, he was the first boy I met with charisma, or so I thought at the time. He looked a bit like a young Angus Deayton, so I fell for his charms in a big way, and we used to sneak a kiss whenever I had to go up to the stock room when no one was looking. He used to take me out for a drink after work, and I was thrilled to be going out with someone a few years older than me. It was all very innocent, just kissing and cuddling, and in fact he taught me how to kiss properly as he said that I kissed like I was kissing a relative. After a few months his friend came into Woolworths to tell me Alan had been engaged for two years and that he was getting married. I was heartbroken and cried for weeks after the news.

I left Woolworths and started a hairdressing apprenticeship. I had worked at a salon when I was fourteen, just shampooing on Saturdays and had enjoyed it very much. Alan's friend started taking me out now and then to take my mind off him. I found it all very exciting because he was in a pop group and had a red sports car too! We went out with each other for three years, and although he was tall, blonde and skinny and not much to look at really, I found him quite exciting to be with. My dad saw right through him from the start, and hated him with a vengeance. When I got pregnant three years later at nineteen, dad tried to talk me out of marrying him, but I wouldn't listen. I thought at the time it was a good opportunity to get away from my controlling dad to be honest and of course I was in love too. Straight out of the frying pan into the fire, I jumped into thirteen years of pure hell. On my Wedding Day I can remember dad saying 'You've made your bed, now lie in it'. I was very hurt when he got up to make his speech at the reception saying 'There are lots of things I would have liked to say at my daughters wedding but I'm afraid I can't say any of them' and then sat down. Thinking back it must have been a terribly worrying time for mum and dad. I'm still not ready to go back down that deep dark hole I called my first marriage, but I hope I can bring myself to talk about it one day, as I feel it would be good therapy for me and may help others too. Just let's say for now that I was lucky to leave the marital home alive.

I went on to have two daughters, Tracy who was born first followed by Michelle seven years later. I must tell you about a visit to mum and dad's house when Tracy was ten and Michelle was three years old. Michelle was quite a handful, and if I didn't insist on holding her hand when we were out she would just run off.

One day during the school holidays, I took Tracy and Michelle to see my mum and dad. They had moved to a large detached house which was on a main road in Worksop, Nottinghamshire and whenever we arrived we always closed the large gates at the top of the long drive behind us, so that if Michelle managed to open the kitchen door onto the drive, at least she wouldn't be able to get to the very busy road. This particular day we were all on the back garden enjoying the sunshine when I heard Michelle open the small gate from the back garden on to the drive. I wasn't all that worried because I knew we had closed the large gates at the top of the drive, but I still got up to see where she was going. Dressed in a vest top and my shorts, I hadn't even bothered to put my flip-flops on as I shouted 'Come back here' to Michelle. When I reached the kitchen door, to my horror I saw Michelle running up the drive, and the gates were open. The postman must have left them open whilst we were on the back garden. The more I shouted to her to come back, the more she ran until she was out of the large gates and near the main road. I ran as fast as I could to grab her quickly as the fast cars and lorries zoomed by, but instead of stopping, Michelle carried on running into the path of the fast flowing traffic, so without thinking of anything else but Michelle, I just ran into the road after her. The cars and lorries swerved and screeched their tyres as their drivers slammed their brakes on sharply, and I felt that we were both going to die as she carried on running towards the woods on the other side of the road where she had seen a kitten playing. When I could almost touch Michelle, a lorry was within an inch of us, and I could feel the heat of its engine and was sure it was going to run over us both. Just at that moment as I looked to my left at the lorry, a mist came over Michelle and me, and it felt like we were being lifted a few inches to the safety of the pavement. As I grabbed her hand, I saw the mist in front of me and realised it was an angel. It wasn't the same angel I had seen before, but it still had a slight smile as it turned and disappeared into the woods.

It truly was a miracle that we were both still alive and that we did not cause a pile up on the busy road. When I got hold of Michelle to pick her up, she still looked full of mischief like she usually did and didn't seem fazed by what had just happened at all. I looked round to see where the angel had gone but she had just disappeared. Michelle got a good telling off when we reached the back garden again, and after that dad used to lock the gates whenever we came to visit, just in case. When I went to bed that evening, I was still very shaken by the whole thing but I thanked the angel for saving our lives because without her I'm convinced we would have both been killed on that road.

A couple of years later I had been so desperate to leave our bungalow with my daughters, then twelve and five years old, that I knocked on the door of my doctors house one morning hoping to speak to his wife to plead with her to help me. At that stage I had never met her before, but she was so kind and understanding, and she certainly did help me, as one week later I was given the keys to a three bedroom council house in the same town I had lived for the last thirteen years in Nottinghamshire. Later I was lucky enough to repay her kindness when I tirelessly helped her with charity work for the local hospital when my girls were a bit older.

I was surprised to discover how spacious my council house was, and set about decorating it with a sense of adventure and hope. I only expected to be living there for about a year or so until my divorce was sorted out, and then I would buy my own house with the proceeds. In the end it took five years before I could buy my own place. I needed peace in my life after my nightmare of a marriage, but peace was not to come until three years later when my next door neighbour from hell finally moved out. My council house was on a pleasant tree lined road in quite a nice area really, and the day I met my next door neighbour was the day I moved in when we said 'Good morning' to each other. I was thirty two then, and she was a bit older with short jet black dyed hair, and she was very short and plump. I was just relieved because she wasn't scruffy looking, and her three children looked clean and tidy too. I told Tracy and Michelle that the first evening in our new home was going to be great, as they helped me put everything away tidily. I was so tired I had asked Tracy to get us some fish and chips from the local chippy whilst I put the kettle on and Michelle laid the table. We had only eaten one mouthful when we nearly choked with fright at the force of the music coming through the walls from next door. Oh, I'd heard loud music before, being married to a musician for thirteen years, but this was something else. We couldn't have heard our television even if we had turned it up full blast. I went round and knocked on their front door for what seemed like ages but no one came. I don't expect that they could even hear me. It went on until midnight, and Tracy and Michelle were very tired when they had to get up for school the next morning and me, well, I hadn't slept a wink all night.

After the girls had gone to school the next morning, I went round to have a chat with my neighbour because I thought that maybe she wasn't aware of how loud the music actually was. It only took a minute for her to laugh in my face and slam her front door shut. Oh hell, what now I thought as I sat in my lounge only to hear what sounded like an electric organ, then a stereo playing something else, plus a television in another room all blasting out through my walls, and then the mad cow went to work leaving it all on. I cried for about an hour, and my head was pounding by this time, so I decided to go to the council offices to make a complaint. They said that they would send an officer round to see me that evening. I couldn't go back home with all the noise going on, so I sat in the park for most of the day just trying to get a bit of peace. When the children came home from school the noise was just as bad, but when the environmental health officer turned up that evening the noise had stopped before he even knocked on my door. He said that he couldn't do anything unless he heard it for himself. It was only when Tracy came home from school the next day that I realised what was happening. She had asked one of the next door neighbours girls who happened to be in her class if she wanted to play after school and the girl replied 'Sorry, I can't, it's my turn to keep watch for anyone coming through your gate, so mum can turn the noise down'. It was disturbing that anyone could be so aggressive and angry, and it was just my luck to be living next door to her.

During the next three years, we did have quiet spells, but we never knew when it would all start up again. On one occasion it all kicked off at 2am one morning, and I did manage to get her attention when I banged on her door with a piece of wood, only for her to be standing there in her nightie and curlers saying she needed someone to talk to because she felt depressed. I stayed there for two hours trying to calm her down, and after that I thought she might be a more considerate neighbour. Over the next two years I never went out on any dates or did any socialising, even though I did get a few offers, because I didn't feel ready for having another man in my life. One weekend my brother David came to do a few jobs for me and stayed the night. It was really peaceful not having to listen to the loud music booming and we all had a pleasant evening. The next morning David went home and I was doing some weeding in the front garden when my neighbours head appeared over my gate. She had an evil look on her face and was pointing her finger in my direction as she said, 'That's her, men coming and going all hours of the day and night'. At that moment another fearsome looking woman with white frizzy hair appeared over my gate shouting and swearing. All this was just because my brother had stayed the night. After that I never ever worried about what people thought of me if that was what you got for being a decent, respectable person.

After three years of her living next door, she finally moved on, and I did get some good neighbours after that. Oh, they still made quite a lot of noise, but it was happy noise. They were a young couple and he used to chase her up the stairs which had no stair carpet, and we would often hear her screaming and laughing. He was quite a joker, and often threatened to get the hosepipe on me when I was sunbathing on the back lawn. The stupid bugger once threw their rabbit over the hedge into our garden when Tracy's rabbit Hopperty was out nibbling grass, and it mounted her and was going at it in the blink of an eye. Tracy loved that rabbit, and was devastated when she went to get Hopperty's dishes to feed her one morning and came running back down the garden sobbing and said that she was stiff and cold and not moving. We put a tea towel in a shoebox and covered her up, and then Tracy insisted on having a funeral at the side of the house before burying her near the dustbin. A kind neighbour gave her some flowers to put on top, and we had to tie two sticks together to make a cross. Even though Tracy is now in her forties she still has dreams about Hopperty now and then.

I never had much money in those days, bringing the children up on my own, but wanted to cheer us all up that weekend, so I raided a jar that I had been saving pennies in, and after counting it I had enough for twenty-one packets of Minstrels, our favourites, so I sent Michelle down the road to get them with this bag of pennies weighing her down. When she came back I asked her who had served her and if they had moaned about having to count the pennies, and she said "No, Sharon said 'Are you having a party then with all these packets of Minstrels', and I said 'No, they are for my mum'". I think it was three weeks before I dared to show my face in the shop out of sheer embarrassment, but when I did go in, we had a good laugh about it.

Chapter 5

After three years of being a single parent, I had grown so much in strength and felt ready to start dating again. I started going out with a friend who used to be a neighbour years ago, and we went for a drink now and then, but I wanted a relationship with someone special. Then one day I spotted an advert in the local newspaper advertising a dating agency called Harmony, so I plucked up the courage to join. I only told mum, Tracy and Michelle. In those days we often used to spend the weekend in Worksop at mum and dads house, and I would look at all the photographs and details of well, it must have been hundreds of men. I was so fed up one weekend that I decided to pluck up the courage to ring someone called John, who was a teacher living in Nottingham. It was hard to see from the photos what any of them looked like, as they were black and white and quite blurred. My heart pounded as I picked up the phone to ring this John, and I could hear my mum and Michelle giggling in the kitchen as my legs shook in the hallway. Dad was mowing the lawn and oblivious to it all, and Tracy had gone shopping. John had a lovely sexy deep voice and I was happily chatting with him for about an hour. Then he asked if I wanted to meet him that evening, and he would pick me up at mum and dads house. When I went back in to the kitchen I said to mum "I can't believe that I've actually arranged to meet a man I've never met before and agreed to have a lift in his car". Mum lent me something to wear because I'd only brought jeans and a jumper as I hadn't dreamed that I would be having a blind date that weekend. It didn't take me long to do my shoulder length hair and put a bit of make-up on early that evening. I wore mums white dress and it fitted me perfectly, and so did her black sling back shoes.

He was picking me up at 8pm. Dad was asleep on the sofa and didn't even know I was going out, let alone with a stranger. It got to about 7:30pm and I was on my fourth visit to the toilet in half an hour, and mum was looking really worried about the whole thing. I had asked her to look through her bedroom window which looked out over the main road and the woodland beyond so that she could look out for his car which he had only described as a yellow one. It got to 7:55pm and my stomach was in knots as I walked into the bedroom, which was in darkness with the curtains open, to see Michelle with dads binoculars round her neck and mum with a notepad and pen she said she had brought up from the kitchen to take his registration number down just in case he didn't bring me back home. I sat on mums bed because my legs were shaking, and then all of a sudden Michelle said "He's here mum, quick he's here" and mum said

"Yes, it's a yellow car, but he's pulled into next doors driveway by mistake, so hurry up before he knocks on their door". I shot past dad, who was by this time in the kitchen doing a crossword, and I quickly said goodbye. I hurried round to next doors drive, and opened the passenger door of a fantastic yellow sports car to see a man with dark hair, but he looked about ten years younger than I expected him to be. I put out my hand to shake hands with him, and said very nervously "I'm Suzanne, pleased to meet you". He looked puzzled and said "Sorry, do I know you, I'm here to pick my mate Tony up to go out for a drink." I wanted the ground to swallow me up as I said "Sorry, there's been a mistake, I do apologise". Dashing past dad, still doing his crossword and looking totally confused by this time, I marched upstairs, threw my handbag on the bed and said 'Right, that's it, I'm not doing this, I can't go through with it'. Mum, Tracy and Michelle thought it was quite amusing, but I was in a terrible state, and then Michelle said that a mustard coloured old car had just pulled up in our driveway. They had to literally throw me out of the front door so I wouldn't have to disturb dad again. As John got out of the car to shake hands with me, I wasn't expecting him to be so good looking. In his forties, tall with a good physique and dark hair greying a little at the sides, I'm not joking when I tell you that he looked like a young Sean Connery when he was playing James Bond. He was dressed in smart grey trousers, a lovely blue shirt and a navy blue v-necked pullover. As he opened the car door for me, I glanced up quickly at mum and dads large imposing house with the lights on in the lounge, hallway and landing, and thought how warm and cosy it looked from the outside. Then I saw the curtain move in mum's bedroom that was still in total darkness, and caught a glimpse of Michelle with the binoculars. I felt alright until John started pulling on his black leather driving gloves very slowly, and panic took over as I felt sure he was planning to murder me and chop me up. Off we went to a lovely country pub not too far away, and I must say in the three hours we spent together I was feeling weak at the knees listening to his deep sexy voice, and felt quite embarrassed when I found myself admiring his muscular physique. I was quite relaxed as we got back to the car and wasn't expecting to be kissed so quickly and expertly. It was very nice though, and the only thing that spoilt the evening for me was when he asked if I wanted to spend the night at his house in Nottingham. I was very relieved when he took me straight back to mum and dads house as requested. Whilst in bed that evening, I thanked my angels for keeping me safe and meeting this very interesting man. We went on to have a lovely relationship for about two years as I recall, although it was a bit upsetting how it ended.

John was spending the bank holiday weekend at my house, and we had gone out for a drink somewhere nice in Derbyshire. I asked him why he had been so quiet all day and he wouldn't say, but after asking him a few times whilst we were out, he just said "Ok then, I don't fancy you any more." I finished my lime and lemon in silence, and the silence continued until we got back to my house. He then took his shoes off, and laying on the sofa with his hands behind his head, he announced that a cup of hot chocolate would be nice. Still in silence I went upstairs, packed his hold-all and threw it on the garden, which was soggy because it was raining heavily by this time. Still lying on the sofa he said "Shut the door will you, it's freezing in here". Picking his shoes up I said "I want you to go NOW", to which he replied "Oh, come on, don't you think you are over reacting a bit here". By now he had got up off the sofa just as I was throwing his shoes out on to the wet garden, and as he went to retrieve them I shut the door on him and lay on the sofa myself. He shouted through the letterbox that he hadn't got enough petrol to get to Nottingham that evening, and with it being bank holiday most of the garages would be shut, as in those days they did not open all day and night. I managed one word; I think it was 'Tough'. Then he shouted "Have you put my shirts in my bag?" After two years together I had started washing and ironing his shirts at the weekends, and had left them hanging on coat-hangers round the outside of my wardrobe. Quick as a flash, I grabbed them with such force that they were totally creased before they hit the garden. His last words through the letterbox were "Thank you, it's been nice!"

I cried for weeks after that, and still to this day I can't believe how hard I was on him that weekend. He did get in touch a few weeks later to say sorry and that he realised he had made a big mistake and could we start again, but for me it was ruined. Thinking back over the years of dating and trying to find my Mr. Right, I realised that John was the only one who had the guts, and in fact the decency to tell me to my face it was over, as I quickly found out that not ringing ever again was the style of the average male, and for that reason alone John and I are still in touch with each other at Christmas time. Only a card and a quick note, but it means a lot to both of us, even though we are both in love with other people now. And what a lucky lady I am to have my kind, respectful and loving husband James, who I have now been married to for eight happy years.

Five years after moving into the council house, I eventually bought a lovely terraced villa in a nice area of the town, not far from where we used to live in the bungalow with my psychopathic ex-husband. Tracy was now seventeen and working as a receptionist for a boat building firm. In those days she had a look of Lady Diana, and was very slim and sophisticated. Michelle was ten and quite a tomboy, but still looked beautiful when she wanted to dress up and would experiment with my lipstick and nail polish whenever I let her.

Chapter 6

When Tracy was twenty-one, she had been going out with her first boyfriend for three years, and they had recently got engaged. A little while after that she had a dodgy cancer smear and had to have laser treatment, and although she was on the pill, the nurse at the clinic forgot to tell her to take precautions straight after the treatment, and four months later she found out she was four months pregnant.. I will never forget the moment when she came home from the family planning clinic after a check up and said "I'm having a baby". The expression on her face was one of fear and happiness rolled into one as she said "I told the nurse you would be pleased when she asked me how you would take it". I was numb before I got to be pleased as I recall, and when her fiancé announced that he didn't even want to commit himself to living together we just had to get on with it.

When Tracy went into early labour, I was at work in a local gift shop when one of her friends came in and asked me to go to the hospital straight away because she had gone into labour. I was in a panic because the baby wasn't due for another nine weeks. I saw the mother of one of Michelle's friends outside the shop, and quickly asked if she would go to Michelle's school (she was fourteen by now), and ask her to bring some things for Tracy to the hospital after school, because I was going straight there. Michelle's friends mum quickly returned just in time to see me leaving the shop to go to the hospital, to tell me that Michelle wasn't at school. It was then that I learnt she played truant now and again. Oh, the joys of being a single parent!

My gorgeous grandson Robert was born in the early hours of the following day weighing only 3lbs 9ozs, and they quickly whisked him off to the Intensive Baby Care Unit. I must admit that I spent more time in those first few days with Robert than Tracy, as she had to stay on the ward for a week I think it was. I couldn't stop looking at him and thinking how lucky I was to have such an adorable grandson. He soon became stronger, and six weeks later he was able to come home. Five months after that, I helped Tracy get a new flat overlooking the park to rent from a local housing association. It seemed quite strange looking out of her window for the first time when I realised that she was born in a flat nearly twenty-two years previously at the other end of the same park. I loved spending time with Tracy and Robert when he was a baby, and still saw a lot of them when Tracy married and went to live a few miles away.

A few years went by and Michelle was working in a fashion shop when she met her first boyfriend. He was in the fashion industry too, and asked her to run a little shop in Belper, Derbyshire for him, so she asked me to help her. He bought her a car when she passed her test, and I was always nagging her to check that she had enough petrol in the car before we got on to the A38 each journey we made, but she would always ask me whose car it was to shut me up. Oh I could cry just thinking of telling you about this particular time when we were going home one evening along the A38. It was dark and the rush hour had started when her car made a spluttering noise and jerked a few times before coming to a halt. In those days mobile phones weren't even invented if I can remember right. We were blocking a lane at the busiest time of the evening and didn't know what to do. Motorists were hooting their horns at us as they went by, but no one stopped to help us. We must have sat in the car for about thirty minutes in that dangerous situation. Michelle was sobbing, and I was so mad with her for running out of petrol, which must have made things worse. Then Michelle said that as the traffic wasn't as busy now, if I got behind the wheel to steer the car, she would try to push it off the road and on to the grass verge. As she was pushing, I heard her scream, and then as I looked in the mirror I saw her jump out of the way and on to the grass verge, and all I could see was headlights lighting up her car, and then the screeching of brakes followed by sparks flying out of the drivers tyres as he franticly tried not to hit her car with me behind the wheel. I heard Michelle screaming for me to jump out of the car, and thinking about it I might have just had the time to, but I felt really warm and the sensation of something hugging me, and as I still looked through the rear view mirror at the sparks flying and the headlights practically upon me, I saw an angel, and it looked like the same angel I had seen when I was unconscious in hospital when I was eleven years old. I could only see her face, but knew I would be alright as the white van behind finally came to a halt. As I took one last look in Michelle's rear mirror, I saw the angel smiling behind me and then it was gone.

The next thing I knew Michelle was opening the car door and asking me if I was alright and hugging me tightly saying "Oh my God, oh my God". When I got out of the car she couldn't believe how calm I was, and as I went to the back of the car and, this is the honest truth, you could have only managed to slide a thin piece of paper between the two bumpers. The rugged looking middle-aged man looked quite shaken as Michelle asked if he could stop at a garage to phone her grandpa, not my dad, my ex-father-in-law, so that he could pick us up. I had a funny feeling about this character when he said that he wouldn't be going near a phone, but said that if Michelle went with him in his van, he would take her to a phone. We asked him if he would help us to push the car out of the inside lane and on to the grass verge, which he did, then off he went and we just sat in the car waiting for someone to help us.

It started to rain heavily, and as the headlights of the cars going by lit up the inside of her car, I could see that her lovely white trousers were covered in dirt from where she had jumped out of the way when the white van was coming towards us. Her hands were shaking and tears streaming down her face as she said that she was dying for the loo. About an hour later, a police car stopped, and the policeman took us to get some petrol and then was kind enough to put it in the car for us. All the way back home

I was thanking my smiling angel for helping us, and saving my life.

A few weeks later, a friend of ours who owned a garage in Derbyshire told Michelle to get rid of the car her boyfriend had bought her because it was what they called a 'cut and shut' and extremely dangerous. Later that year I was lucky enough to see the angel again and actually find out who she was.

Yes, it was the same year as the A38 episode, and I had just returned from a six mile walk which I often used to do just for pleasure, and to keep me fit too. I wish I could still do long walks now, but unfortunately I can't. As I was taking my coat off, dad rang to ask me something. It wasn't very often that we spoke on the phone, or if we did it was only when I rang mum, and he would answer and briefly say "I'll get your mum". I told him where I had been walking and he said that I must have gone past the cemetery where my great grandma and grandpa were buried; they were the parents of my beloved grandad who I spent most of my school holidays with, and I still miss him and grandma very much. A few days later, I decided to visit my great grandparents grave as I was walking that way anyway. The old church was in a very pretty little village with flowering cherry trees lining the roadside, and as I walked up the path leading to the church, I passed gravestones that were so old I just knew they would even be before my great grandparents time. As I stood to admire the beautiful old church from outside, I spotted another path which led to the cemetery. I took my time and read every gravestone but I just couldn't find theirs, then as I made my way to the side of the church I spotted another cemetery just through some trees and round a corner. This area was very run down with weeds and long grass covering many of the headstones, but I was on a mission to find the grave, so I started at the far end and waded through the long grass moving weeds to one side to read the inscriptions on the stones. I was fascinated with all the old names, some I hadn't even heard of and some that made me smile. When I had searched about half of the old cemetery, I became aware of how lonely it was with not seeing anyone passing by all the time I was there, and I must admit I then felt quite vulnerable in this isolated spot. Just at that moment I spotted a large black marble headstone, much larger than any of the others, and I was drawn to it for some reason. The black marble had beautiful gold lettering, and as I read it I realised it was the one that I had been looking for. William had died in 1933, and Elizabeth had died in 1940, seven years before I was born. Tears filled my eyes as I looked at the grave which had sunk down about two feet, and huge nettles and thistles were growing from its depths. I was so sad that although I had never met them, they were still my family and I was ashamed of the state it was in. I used a few of my wet wipes to remove the bird mess on the headstone and was amazed how the lettering had stayed so clear after all those years. It got me thinking that with my great grandpa dying first, Elizabeth must have chosen the grand headstone which looked the best in the cemetery. I had heard my dad saying on many occasions what a proud lady she was, so to me it was even sadder to see the state it was in now. I found a black marble pot with mesh on the top that you put flowers in which was on the ground a few feet away, and placed it back near the headstone as I whispered to my great grandparents that I would sort the grave out for them, with the tears still rolling down my face. As I was walking back towards the church, I spotted the vicar and asked him if it was alright to do some work on the grave as soon as I found someone to take it on, and he assured me he would be more than happy for improvements to be made. When I returned home, I rang a local builder who had done some work to my house a few months previously, and asked him to come with me to the grave to see if he could do anything to make it better. The builder rang a few weeks later to say he was picking me up that afternoon to show me what he had done. I took a big bunch of flowers with me from the nearby petrol station and put them in the black marble vase, and then stepped back in disbelief as the large black marble headstone shone in the sunlight. It looked like a brand new grave with green pebbles on top of the concrete the builder had filled the sunken grave in with, and the pink roses, carnations and white gypsophlia in the vase. When I got back home I went to bed as I had a very bad cold and felt quite weak. A couple of weeks later I was still full of cold when I woke up about 4am. I didn't bother putting the light on, but sat up in bed feeling round for the hanky that I had been holding when I went to sleep at 9pm the night before. I was just about to blow my nose when at the bottom of my bed I saw a lady with long grey hair dressed in white with a mist all around her, and as the mist moved, it appeared that she had misty looking wings. I can remember feeling calm and not at all afraid as I said "Who are you?". I had to pinch my arm really hard just to check if I was awake or not, and I was aware of the sound of some traffic going by on the main road where I lived. I even pinched my nose hard when I was blowing it just to make sure I was definitely awake. She smiled slightly and started moving very slowly towards me, it was like she was floating. When she got to about a foot away from me, I can remember thinking to myself 'Where is she going?', and then I spotted her pale blue eyes, the same colour eyes the angel I had seen before had. She started rising slowly, and as I was gazing up at her she gently turned upside down like she was standing on her head, but in mid air. Then all of a sudden she started coming downwards until her head was touching mine. As she slowly disappeared, all I could feel was a flutter in my stomach like when you have just driven over a bridge quickly. I got up, went to the loo, and then just went back to sleep. When I got up later and went to the bathroom to have a wash and clean my teeth, I noticed nail marks where I had pinched my nose and could see the marks where I had pinched my arm at 4am to check if I was awake or not. I felt really calm and happy that this angelic lady had chosen to visit me, and was surprised that the cold I had been suffering from was now completely gone. I can't even say that the whole experience was down to any medication I had taken for my cold, because I hadn't taken anything. It was only three weeks later that I was to see those lovely pale blue eyes again.

We loved mum and dad's big old house in Worksop, Nottinghamshire; the large dining room had double French doors that opened onto a patio and the huge lawn with not a weed in sight. Above the radiator on the far wall there were two old fashioned oval picture frames with a photograph of a man in one and a lady in the other. They had been there for about a year, but I hadn't asked who they were because I knew dad would have gone on and on for hours explaining about it all. They seemed to appear on mum and dad's wall when my grandads sister died because I can remember the same photographs hanging in her front room when I used to visit her, but even then I had never taken much notice of them. Usually whenever I sat at mum and dad's dining table for a meal, I would sit with my back to the photographs anyway so that I could be near the radiator, but this particular day I was a bit hot after helping mum cook the Sunday lunch and decide to sit on the opposite side of the table instead. I was just about to put my first fork full of food into my mouth, when my eyes got locked on to the eyes of the lady in the photograph opposite me. She looked very regal in her cream high necked frilly long sleeved blouse and her dark hair done up elegantly in a bun. She had been posing sideways with her eyes looking into the camera, just as I do when I'm having my photograph taken. Her eyes were the same eyes as the lady who had visited me at the bottom of my bed a few weeks previously and there was no mistaking that beautiful face, yes it was the very same face. I stared at the photograph for what seemed like ages, and mum had asked me twice if I was alright. I turned to dad and said "Who is that lady in the photograph?", and he said "Oh, that's your great grandma, the one whose grave you did up a few weeks ago". I didn't eat my meal that day. I just stared at her photograph and knew then she was my guardian angel. It's funny but I once read an angel book about meditation and during it, I was supposed to concentrate and ask my guardian angel what her name was and all that kept coming to me was Elizabeth, and that just happens to be my great grandma's name. My grandad had the same colour eyes as his mum, and my lovely grandson Robert and beautiful baby granddaughter Keira do too!

Chapter 7

I was in my late thirties when I got a part-time job as a receptionist with a double glazing firm and decided to work behind the bar at a lovely country pub on the outskirts of Derbyshire. As I didn't have a social life, I thought at least it would get me out and meeting people, and perhaps hopefully find romance with someone nice. I instantly made friends with Margaret and Jean on my very first shift there. Margaret was a voluptuous blonde about my age who was always laughing and joking and a joy to be with. It was a nice surprise when her husband Vic came to pick her up at the end of the evening and I discovered we were in the same class at school together. Jean on the other hand was a widow who was slightly older than me, a very elegant attractive brunette with a dry sense of humour. Jean and I are still in touch to this day and she often makes me laugh when we are talking about the old days on the phone and I value her friendship dearly. I haven't heard from Margaret for years now, but Jean does occasionally and keeps me up to date. After I had been working at the pub for a few months, I decided to have a holiday at a resort near Barcelona in northern Spain.

When at home I always went to bed at 9pm when I wasn't working, but I seemed to change completely once there and would have a sleep in the late afternoon, then a late evening meal and go to the Western Bar until about 2am. I never drank alcohol back at home, but when on holiday I liked to have Pernod with blackcurrant and lemonade, and even plucked up the courage to have a dance. Before I went off on this particular holiday, I can remember my friend Margaret saying that I had got to let my hair down and live a bit whilst I was still young enough. So off I went on holiday with another friend, who was younger than me. We had met whilst working together and had then kept in touch when we had both found different jobs. I used to love sunbathing all day and then going to the Western Bar in the evening until the early hours. I used to enjoy dressing up and felt quite glamorous in those days. They knew us at the bar and would greet us with a hug, and whenever I went without Michelle they would always ask about her because she used to enjoy it when I took her too, as children were allowed in until a certain time.

Sitting at the bar this particular evening, I caught Frank's eyes on me every time I looked up. He was half English and half Spanish, and was always working behind the bar whenever I went there. He was quite handsome in a rugged sort of way, with jet black shoulder length hair and he was quite tall and masculine. He always seemed to be wearing a vest as did all the other lads behind the bar, but he always looked more fitter than them. Sitting at the bar which had a western theme going on, there was a bull not far behind me in the corner that you had to try and stay on for as long as you could as it threw you one way and then another. I never ever went on it, but Michelle had done a few times and was rather good at it actually. Over the other side of the bar, which was square shaped, there was quite a large area to have a dance and on the wall was the huge screen showing videos of pop stars. The music used to be quite loud which for some reason didn't seem to bother me whilst I was there. The coloured flashing lights around the dance area and bar seemed to add to the electric atmosphere.

I thought Frank would have given up asking me to go to a nightclub with him after he had finished work, because I always used to laugh and say no to him. I had never been to a night club before and must admit I was tempted. After his mates reassured me that they would have a word with him to act like a gentleman, and him telling me that I would enjoy it and he would behave himself, I don't know if it was the Pernod or Margaret's words going round my head telling me to let my hair down and live a bit, but I found myself saying "Ok then, I will".

I walked back to the hotel just across the road with my friend, as she wanted to go to bed because she had a headache, and I spent about an hour in the hotel room with her before going back to the bar. She assured me that I would be alright when I started to get cold feet about the whole thing and said "Let your hair down for once and enjoy yourself". Off I went like a lamb to the slaughter in my favourite black strappy dress. It was like a chiffon material, and from the waist it hung loosely to just below the knee. I always got lots of compliments whenever I wore it, so it gave me extra confidence. It seemed weird for me to be walking across the road from the hotel to the Western Bar at 1.30am in the morning alone. Oh I've done some stupid things in my time, and apart from marrying my ex-husband this one beats the lot.

As I crossed the road it was still very busy with lots of people enjoying themselves. My heart thumped at the thought of walking into the Western Bar alone. I had a chat with one of Frank's mates as he gave leaflets out just outside the entrance to the bar, and he assured me they had all had a chat with Frank and he told them he would take me to a night club for an hour or so and would bring me back to the hotel straight afterwards and that he would behave himself. Down the steps I went into the busy bar and Frank kissed my hand as I sipped another Pernod. It wasn't long before he took hold of my hand and said "Let's go and hit the clubs" as I replied "Oh, I only want to go to one because I've never been to a night club before". I found it exciting when he spoke in Spanish to a few people outside a couple of clubs only to let me know afterwards that they were closed. Down the hill we walked until we turned off the main street into an area I didn't know at all and yet again we found more clubs just closing. At this point I remember asking him to take me back to the hotel and saying that we could go to a club another night instead, only to be told there was just one more round the corner to try. I started to feel a bit panicky because I didn't know where we were, when all of a sudden he said in his half Spanish half English accent "Come, it's here" as we walked towards a large old building with huge doors. I told him that it must be closed because I couldn't hear any music and asked him again to walk me back to the hotel. My voice sounded a bit shaky by this time and my stomach was churning as the effects of the Pernod, which had given me a bit of courage earlier quickly began to wear off. As we stood in front of these huge doors, which were half open, he grabbed my hand as he opened a door just inside the entrance and pushed me inside as he switched the light on. Shaking with fright and my heart thumping so loudly I could hear and feel every beat, I quickly scanned the room which was more like a cupboard as it was so small. It had twin beds, one of which was broken in a heap, and both beds touched a wall either side with about four inches between them, and there was a filthy sink in the corner near the door.

I started shouting at him and saying that he had told me he was taking me for a drink and that was all. He then pushed a bottle of whisky at me after he had had a swig first. I shouted "Take me back to the hotel now Frank, please", but he lunged at me and as he tried to kiss me, he ripped one of the straps off my lovely black dress as he attempted to rip it off me. I felt like I had died and gone to hell as he forcefully pushed me on to the filthy bed. As I struggled to even breathe with the weight of him upon me, quick as a flash he had ripped my little black lacy pants down to my ankles. I could smell his sweaty armpits as he tried to hold one of my arms above my head whilst fumbling to get his manhood out of his shorts with the other. As I felt him trying to push it inside my trembling body, I just thought no way is this going to happen to me, as I brought my other hand down between us both very sharply and he shouted out in pain. I reached down and picked one of my shoes up from the floor, which had somehow fallen off as he pushed me on to the bed seconds earlier, and I struck him twice on the head with it. As he released his weight from me and rolled over, I grabbed my other shoe and handbag, and quickly tried to open the door to escape, but the door wouldn't open. As I tried again franticly, and with my lacy pants hanging off the shoe in my hand because I didn't have time to put them on when I grabbed the other shoe from the floor, quick as a flash he grabbed hold of my short hair from the back and tried to force me back on the bed, but I brought my knee up quickly and heard him groaning as I made another dash for the door. This time it opened and I hid behind a piece of furniture in the grand hallway to put my pants on quickly before running into the street.

By this time it must have been about 3am, because we had walked for quite a while supposedly looking for a night club to have a drink. I didn't know what direction to go in because I was totally lost. I spotted a café next door to the large building and saw two old men having a drink at the back with the lights dimmed, and started banging on the door shouting for help whilst holding the top of my dress up, but one of them came to the door, spat on the floor and pulled the shutters down. I looked to my right and saw some phone boxes the other side of what looked like the market and started walking towards them to try and phone the police, but as I made my way over the square I saw small groups of Spanish youths squatting in shop doorways either looking drunk or off their heads with drugs.

As a group of them staggered towards me, I ran in the opposite direction, realising that what had just happened with Frank was a picnic compared with what else could happen to me as I tried to find my way back to the hotel. As I ran, I spotted a decent looking young man who had just pulled up to park his car after a night out, and before he got out of his car I banged on his window. As he wound it down, I begged him to take me back to my hotel and reached in my handbag for some money to pay him. The poor lad didn't speak very much English at all and looked horrified when I kept saying "hotel, hotel" and pushing money at him, until I started crying and he realised I was in trouble. I was in such a state by this time I couldn't even remember the name of the hotel I was staying at when he asked me in very poor English. So I pointed in the direction I thought the seafront was and hoped I would realise where I was, so that I could get my bearings and tell him the road back to my hotel from there. He got out and opened the car door for me as he said "I try to help you, I try to help you" to calm me down a bit, but it was a while before I realised we were going the wrong way and I quickly kept repeating "Sea front, sea front". He looked puzzled but did as I asked, and once I saw the sea it didn't take me long to get my bearings again as I pointed up the hill to the hotel. He was just pulling up near my hotel where a large group of rowdy youths were gathered on the pavement singing and shouting when I offered him the equivalent of about twenty pounds, because I was so grateful to him for giving me a lift back.

Just at that moment, like a bat out of hell, his girlfriend, who had been asleep on the back seat and entirely un-noticed by me, lunged at me from behind and pulled my head backwards with my hair, and then tried to strangle me whilst shouting and screaming in Spanish. The young man tried to get her off me, shouting back in Spanish to her and trying to explain himself as she threw her arms in the air and flicked her hands one way then another, and even tried to have another go at me before finally calming down and smiling at me as she patted my shoulder and said "Sorry, I sorry ok". They waved as I made my way towards the hotel and then hooted the horn as they drove off. I walked by the drunken youths on the pavement, who whistled as I walked up the steps to the hotel, but as I tried to open the main doors, to my horror they were locked. "Oh God no", I said out loud as I banged on the door in the hope that someone would hear me. I heard the youths on the pavement shouting "Come here darling", and as I looked round in fright, a few of them were making their way up the steps. Banging so hard on the glass doors had made my knuckles bleed and I was crying out "Lord help me, please help me", when all of a sudden the doors opened then closed behind me and I more or less collapsed with relief as I looked round to thank whoever it was who let me in, but there was no one in sight.

By this time, the youths had their noses pressed to the glass doors trying to get in, but the doors were locked. Looking round in amazement, I made my way to the stairs to get to the fourth floor, but instead of walking up it felt like I was being carried up, and I felt a warm glow inside me. Once inside our room, my friend had mumbled "What time is it?" and I told her to go back to sleep. I went into the bathroom, started running a bath, and then sat on the toilet seat sobbing and shaking. I think I had seven baths in the next two hours before I collapsed into bed. When I told my friend the next morning, she said that I must go to the Police Station, but I needed to rest and think about it. I asked the receptionist on duty after breakfast to thank whoever let me in when I was banging on the doors, and she asked what time it happened. I told her it must have been about 3:30 or 4am, and she said that there was no one around then because they lock the doors at 2am. I knew then that I had been let in and carried up the stairs by an Angel!

I decide not to contact the police about the incident, but instead decided to tell all his mates and workmates, including his boss. After this I continued to visit the bar with my friend in the evenings, because I felt I wasn't the one who had done anything wrong. For the rest of the holiday, I noticed that Frank's workmates were making his life hell, and he actually apologised to me for his behaviour before we flew home, so I felt that there was some closure to it in a way.

Chapter 8

I would like to tell you now about a picture I saw when I was in my forties and living in Nottinghamshire. Being a single parent of my two girls, I didn't have much money in those days, so a lot of the time was spent window shopping rather than buying anything. After walking through the shopping centre, one day I decided to pop into the indoor market to buy some fruit. Just before I got to the entrance, I decided to stop and look in my purse to see if I'd got enough money for what I was about to buy, when I found myself opposite a glass showcase displaying paintings by a local artist. I put my purse back in my handbag and was about to walk into the market when my eyes were drawn to one of the half dozen or so paintings on display. It was a picture of an old mill, trees and water in Derbyshire somewhere, but there was something about this picture that left me spellbound, and I must have been staring at it for about half an hour or so, and even when I had been into the market to buy my fruit, I had to go back to this oil painting again. I had never shown much interest in paintings before, but there was something very special about this one. I sighed as I walked away, knowing that I could not afford to pay the two hundred pounds being asked for it, but every time I went shopping I would go and look at my painting, as I called it.

During the next two years my heart would sink if ever the painting had been replaced by another one, because each time I would think it had been sold and I wouldn't see it again. Weeks later it would reappear for me to admire, and my heart would skip a beat at the sight of it again. I couldn't understand why I felt this way about it, but this went on for two years, until I could stand it no longer and went to the bank to ask for a two hundred pound loan so that I could buy the picture. To my surprise the bank manager said yes, so I called into the fashion shop that Michelle worked in at the time to tell her my news, but she looked really annoyed and said that I had ruined her surprise. Apparently, because I had been going on about the painting for two years, she had been saving up to buy it for me as a birthday present. I rang the artist to arrange to buy the painting, and had agreed with Michelle that she could pay half towards it, but to my horror it had been sold that morning to a gentleman who lived miles away. I cried for most of that day with a heavy heart, but about 6pm that same evening the door bell rang and it was the local artist standing there with a big smile on his face. Earlier in the day he had told me that he would paint me another picture similar to the one I had seen, but I had been really adamant that it was the one I had been looking longingly at for two years that I wanted. Apparently he had contacted the buyer and told him about my love of it, and the buyer let me have it as he had seen another one he had liked that day and was happy to have that instead, so here was the artist at my door after going to retrieve my special picture for me. I hung it in my dining room and a few weeks later mum and dad came for Sunday lunch. Mum noticed the picture and said "Oh that looks like my dad's mill that he had in Cromford, Derbyshire." I told her that the artist had said when he brought it to my door that it was of a mill in Cromford. In the end it wasn't my grandpas mill, but one very close to where his was. I had never really known him as he died when I was very young and no one ever spoke of him. It was years later at mum and dads house that I found out more about my grandpa.

He had been a very wealthy man and had brought lots of employment to the town of Matlock, and he was very well respected in those days, but then he had apparently started to gamble and lost quite a lot of money. It sounds like he took his anger out on my lovely gran and hit her for the first time. Gran was a pretty, elegant and slim lady with style and extremely kind too. She went to the doctor to ask his advice as he was also a friend of the family and he told her that if her husband hit her again, she could have him put in a mental home if she got another doctor to sign the papers as well, and that's what she did and he stayed there until he died. Oh, bring back the old days I say, my ex-husband would have been there like a shot! When my ex-husband hit me I went to the Police Station in fear of my life, and was told it was a domestic so they couldn't do anything, and in the sixties and seventies there wasn't anywhere to go then, as far as I know.

After my near death experience in Plymouth that led me to live in Looe and go on to write my first book 'Smiling Angels', a lady who had bought my book from Angels Wings in Looe not long after it was published went back to the shop to ask the assistant if she could pass a message on to me. The lady lived in Lincolnshire I think she said and had gone home now after a weeks holiday in Looe. She said that she wasn't a medium or anything but that she had had a strange experience whilst reading my book. I had been saying for a few weeks that I must have been getting some help from someone after my books had been selling so quickly, and after the message I knew who it was. The lady said that all the time she was reading my book, the vision of a pear kept coming to her. The experience was so intense for her that she felt compelled to pass it on to me.

When my mum was seventy-six she had a heart attack and a stroke whilst getting up in the early hours to catch a plane to Turkey for one of her many holidays, and whilst she was in hospital she wasn't able to have anything to eat or drink for a few days, until my brother Ron and I managed to talk the doctor into giving her a drink. He said she wouldn't be able to manage it, but she did and even progressed to having milk. Mum managed to speak a few words although her speech was quite slurred and said "When I get out of here I'm going to have a nice juicy pear". Unfortunately mum had another stroke just as I was about to give her some food and sadly died the next evening. Ever since then, more than ten years ago now, my sister and I have bought pears every week and put them in a fruit bowl in our kitchens in memory of mum. So when the lady who read my book had the strange vision of a pear, I knew it was a message from mum telling me it was her helping me sell so many books. I was very grateful for the lady passing that message on to Angels Wings but I'm afraid I don't even have her name and address to thank her, but hopefully she might buy this book and know that it was very special to me.

Since my near death experience in Plymouth, almost eleven years ago now, I have had a few unusual things happen to me, when the feeling that I have lived before has come over me. It's happened about four times, the first one being when I first ever set eyes on Looe in Cornwall after my near death experience which I told you about in my first book 'Smiling Angels'. The second time was when we went on a return visit to the Dominican Republic in 2004. James and I had been to the Bahia Maimon resort for our honeymoon in 2001and stayed at the Riu Merengue, a luxury all inclusive hotel complex on a white sandy beach. Like on a lot of foreign holidays, we saw signs of poverty as we made our way from the airport to the hotel by coach, but I had not expected it to be as bad as what we experienced there. It's very upsetting and always makes me feel so lucky and privileged for the good life I am fortunate enough to be living. It was like stepping into another world as the coach approached some huge iron gates with guards standing either side holding what looked like machine guns. As we got off the coach and went up the steps to the open main reception area, we realised straight away that we were not going to be disappointed. The huge flower arrangement in the centre of the reception area was magnificent. I'd never seen anything like it before. The cream marble floor was spotless, with a few marble pillars here and there, beautiful wicker furniture with brightly coloured cushions, and there must have been at least ten receptionists with their white teeth gleaming as they greeted us warmly. We could see the turquoise sea and the beautiful white sands just beyond the kidney shaped swimming pool with a small bridge over it leading to a large thatched roof building on the other side.

We were taken to our room which was a few hundred yards away, and as we walked the mango tree lined paths and beautiful tropical gardens with flowers I'd never even seen before waving in the breeze, James held my hand and I just knew our honeymoon would be perfect. The rooms were in blocks of eight, four up and four down with lush gardens in between the next lot of buildings and we were shown to ours which was on the lower floor. We couldn't believe how luxurious it was with brightly coloured curtains to two huge windows either side, two king sized beds with throw-overs to match the curtains, wicker furniture, huge wardrobes and a spacious en-suite. When we opened the patio doors there was more beautiful wicker furniture, and as we sipped the champagne on the terrace which had been left in an ice bucket in our room for us, the blue sky and magnificent sunshine made it feel like paradise. The sight and sounds of the unusual birds, the lizards climbing up palm trees and bananas growing just inches away from our terrace were all part of this magical place.

We walked back through the main reception en route to the dining room for our evening meal, and just as we went by a few shops near the dining room, some huge doors suddenly opened and out came waiters and waitresses dressed in brightly coloured shirts and blouses, singing and clapping as people started making their way into the enchanting dining room. The sea was so close we could smell and hear it as we sat down at our table to eat the starters we had chosen at the buffet style restaurant. We could see boats on the water, people on jet-skis and there were still some people lying on the beach as it was only 6:30pm. We had chosen first sitting for our evening meal as the next one was about 9pm, and we don't like to eat that late. Nelson our waiter couldn't have looked after us more, and the food was unbelievable, with the choices seeming to be never ending and so expertly cooked too. It wasn't long before the hotel's singing trio started going from table to table serenading people whilst the guests ate and sipped wine by candle light. When they came to us we looked up at them and smiled, but one of them told us in broken English to carry on eating whilst they played. There was one tall thin man with a moustache playing a guitar, one old man who looked as if he might not make it to the end of the song which was 'Yellow Bird', and a very short pigeon chested man with grey hair playing the maracas. They were out of tune, and

I found it quite amusing as I struggled with a fit of the giggles. I was trying to hold back and kicked James under the table a few times, which only made matters worse because that set him off as he nearly choked trying not to laugh. 'Yellow Bird' seemed to go on for an hour but I'm sure in reality it was only minutes. Later on we strolled through the gardens and found a whole street of lovely shops that stayed open until 10pm every evening, and we explored every one at our leisure. We walked a bit further in the opposite direction and found another hotel which was the sister hotel to ours, and had a few fruit cocktails before skipping all the entertainment in favour of an early night; well, we were on our honeymoon after all!

The next day, after an unbelievable breakfast of mango juice, bacon and eggs, and pancakes with maple syrup followed by coffee and doughnuts, we realised our stomachs couldn't cope and soon got into a routine of sensible eating with me having fruit every morning, and James spoilt for choice with his muesli. Later on that day as I lay on my stomach on a sun bed, with the hot sun beating down on me, someone tapped me on the shoulder and I looked up to see a big local lady towering over me asking if I wanted a massage. She dragged my sun bed under some palm trees and gave me a thorough massage, including my face, head and fingers, and although she was a bit rough at times especially when doing my back, I thoroughly enjoyed the whole experience and couldn't believe it when, after an hours vigorous massage, she only charged me the equivalent of four pounds in English money! Later on that day, we went for a stroll and found a smaller beach where we could try out the water sports if we wanted, and not far away were some wooden shacks where locals were selling jewellery and ornaments. One young man shouted to me "Hey lady, come inside" as we strolled by a shack with pottery outside the door, and as I smiled and shook my head whilst still walking, he said "Come on lady, I Mr. Cheapy" which made me laugh, so we went inside to have a browse. Afterwards I lay on a sun bed under a tree because I was in need of a bit of shade with the hot sun beating down on me, and James had gone to the waters edge to watch people getting ready to set off on jet-skis as he contemplated whether to have a go or not. A few minutes later, I didn't feel worried when I felt the weight of something on the bottom of my sun bed, and didn't even open my eyes because I thought it was James sitting there. A few seconds later I said "Stop messing about on my bed, you are in my sun", but as I opened my eyes I was gripped with fear to see a large dog looking into my eyes and straddled over my body. It looked a bit like an Irish Wolfhound and belonged to one of the local workers. I have always been quite scared of dogs after one bit me when I was a child. I raised my head slightly to one side and the dog started to lick my face. A few people sunbathing a few yards away had seen the dog and were laughing at the expression on my face. I was very relieved when the dog clambered off my sun bed, and was hoping it would go back to its owner, but it decided to settle down on the sand by my sun bed and went to sleep.

We had a wonderful honeymoon there and have very happy memories of the place, so in 2004 we decided to go again and stay at the same hotel. Everything looked the same as it was before when we arrived and even Nelson, our waiter from before, recognised us and gave me a kiss. In fact the only thing that had changed was that they had built a new hotel on the complex. It had been built at the end of the street of shops about ten minutes walk from our hotel, so one day when it was cloudy we decided to have a stroll to this new hotel and have a coffee there. We sat on a sofa that was so soft and comfy I wondered how we were going to get up again, as we watched people coming and going. After sitting there for about half an hour, it was pretty quiet in the reception area as James and I contemplated moving on. As I looked up I spotted a lady with a large broom sweeping the floor. She was about my age, but was so thin and gaunt looking she looked like someone who was about to die. She came a little closer to where we were sitting and our eyes locked together as she was giving me a beaming smile. I had tears rolling down my face as James asked me what was wrong, but I couldn't speak or take my eyes off this lady until she disappeared round a corner. I went to the toilet just off the main reception, and as I was coming out she was sweeping near the door and gave me another beaming warm smile. I was overwhelmed with the feelings I had when looking into this ladies eyes, and when I got back to James I said "Please don't laugh at me, but that cleaning lady was my mother in another life". When he asked me how I knew that, I said "Believe me, I know". I was relieved when he didn't laugh at me, and I sat in the reception area for about an hour every day after that hoping to catch a glimpse of her to see if the same overwhelming feelings came over me, but I never saw her again. I can't explain it, but I just knew she was my mother in another life, just as I knew I had lived before in Looe in Cornwall after I had my near death experience in 1998.

The third unusual thing to happen to me was about four years ago when I was shopping in Plymouth with James. I was drawn to some Indians playing the most wonderful pipe music outside Dingles department store, and every now and then they did a little dance, shaking what looked like maracas. I couldn't take my eyes off them and sat on a wall for about two hours, just listening to the music and watching them, although it only seemed like minutes to me. I bought two of the CD's that they were selling and my favourite tune is 'Return of the Mohicans', and I had a strong feeling that I had lived a life like them before, but it wasn't until they returned again two years later to Plymouth that I had a much stronger feeling, a very overwhelming feeling. Once again I was drawn to the music as I went from one shop to another, until I eventually found them outside W. H. Smiths this time. Three young men were dressed in brown tasselled jackets and trousers, and were dancing now and then as they played pipes and maracas. I was drawn to one young man in particular and couldn't take my eyes off him as he danced around, and then a strong vision came into my head that I had lived a life with Indians and lost a young child in that life. It was such a strong and overwhelming feeling that I started sobbing as I sat on a wall watching him. After about an hour I walked away because I didn't have a lot of time, but after a few minutes I had to return, and I'm not joking that if one of them had held out his hand and said "Come on I'm taking you home where you belong", in that split second I would have gone back into the life I thought I had lived before as an Indian!

Until my near death experience in Plymouth, I had never experienced those unusual feelings of living in another lifetime before, and my daughter Michelle and her friend said that I should have past life regression with a hypnotist. I thought no more about it until I was in Truro waiting to see my acupuncturist in the reception area at a natural therapy centre in 2008. A young lady walked in who worked there and commented on what a large bright aura I had, and after discovering that she was a hypnotist and also did past life regression, I impulsively made an appointment, out of curiosity really. Well, they say 'Curiosity killed the cat' and if I'd known that I was going to remember everything afterwards I would never have had the hypnosis at all.

When the day of my appointment arrived, I recall being nervous but more excited than anything. The young woman called my name when I was sitting in the reception area, and my heart skipped a beat as I wondered if I had indeed lived any lives before this one. The young hypnotist was pretty with short dark hair, and she assured me that she had done past life regression on many clients, and just to relax and enjoy it. It was then she told me that I would be aware

I was on the bed throughout the session and could ask her to stop at any time. After the usual relaxation technique of imagining your body bit by bit getting heavier and more relaxed, she told me to think of a lovely place and imagine myself there. She told me afterwards that she thought I would have picked a beach somewhere hot or something like that, but I found myself in this old house where I saw unusual clocks and furniture, but I felt I belonged there as my mind went from room to room. She then told me to imagine a beautiful garden with every sort of flower I have ever seen, and with a large lawn and a gate at the bottom. I must admit I was struggling to imagine this garden, because my mind wanted to stay in the lovely old house where I felt I belonged. I'm sure if she had asked me questions about that house I could have told her about my life in it many years ago, but I eventually imagined this garden and was told to go through the gate at the bottom and along a path through some woods and down some steps, counting them as I stepped down. I then went through another wood and down some steps to a bridge, counting very slowly as I went down.

At that stage I was still slightly aware that I was on the bed with the hypnotist talking to me, and I was aware of traffic going by on the busy road outside. Once on the bridge, I was asked to look into the water and watch all the people I had known in my past lives go by, and wish them well. I remember thinking how stupid it was as I couldn't see any peoples faces in the water at all. I was then asked to imagine a mist coming over the bridge and to walk through the mist to the other end. I was then asked to step off the bridge and out of the mist, and I was asked what I was seeing and where I was.

I couldn't believe what was coming out of my mouth as I said "I'm in York, it's the year 1600 and my name is Molly. I am driving a cart of apples to market." I told her I was thirty years of age and, if asked, I would have said I had a daughter called Alice, but she didn't ask me. As the session went on, I told of seeing a beautiful lady stepping out of a carriage with buttons on her fine shoes, and wearing a long dress and a pretty bonnet. I described the coach drawn by two black horses, and gentlemen passing by with top hats and long black coats or cloaks. I told of pointed tall buildings that were practically leaning into each other, and they looked like they had been in a fire with their charred appearance. Later I told of being in the market place in York, which had lavender on display together with dead pigs hanging up and geese running round. Whilst I was in the market place, men put chains on me and dragged me away. They took me to a dungeon with smelly filthy people with matted hair and black teeth laughing at me, as I was thrown in with them. I could smell and feel everything as they pushed me around. When asked by the hypnotist what I had done wrong, I told her that I hadn't done anything and they must have the wrong person. Later on I told of a hanging gallows in a yard and being dragged to it by two men. I was sobbing as people were cheering and throwing bad fruit at me, as they placed the noose around my neck. I was asked if I wanted to stay to the end but I said no, so the hypnotist told me to step back on to the bridge and into the mist again.

Just as before I was asked to step off the bridge again and out of the mist and asked what I could see. Once again I couldn't believe what was coming out of my mouth as I told her that I was in a canyon on a horse. Yes, this time I was a Sioux Indian on a brown and white horse and I was on my way to hunt buffalo. When asked what my name was by the hypnotist, I replied "Little Horse", and then remember thinking 'What am I saying?' At that moment, I can remember thinking my grandson Robert would probably say "What a load of rubbish", and I must admit that I couldn't understand why the words were coming out of my mouth so freely. I described going home to my family and the smells of cooking outside on the fires filling my nostrils, with skins of all shapes and sizes hanging out to dry, and children playing. I told of my father being Chief and not in good health, then of a medicine man dancing round him before he finally died. I can remember being on the bed and crying because he had died, and the hypnotist asking me how I felt about him dying. I said that I was worried because I was Chief now and didn't feel ready, and told of the hard life the Sioux Indians live.

She asked me to fast-forward my life to near the end, and I said that I was on my horse with many others of my tribe and being shot in the shoulder and then in the head by men in blue uniforms. I told of falling off my horse, but no one had seen me fall, and I was left on my own on the ground with the burning sun beating down on me. I told of excruciating pains in my head and feeling very ill and lonely. The hypnotist asked me if I wanted to stay to the end, and when I said no she asked me to step on to the bridge again and into the mist. When she asked me if I wanted to step into another life I said "No thanks, I want to come back" so she counted me up the steps and through the woods and garden, and then through the beautiful place she had originally asked me to imagine, which was the lovely old house I had found myself in. My thoughts lingered there as I went from room to room, and I know that I could have told a story of that house if she had asked me to.

As I got off the bed, I was shocked that I could remember everything about the two hour session I had just had, and after telling a few friends about it, and my husband James looking at me as if I'd got three heads, I decided the best thing to do was to just forget about the whole thing, which I did until I have told you about it. Of course James told my grandson Robert, and he nearly cracked up laughing at me. It's certainly cured my curiosity, and I will not be having it again thank you very much. I do believe in reincarnation, but with the past life regression therapy, well I don't really know how it works, so I'm putting that down to deep imagination whilst in an induced state of relaxation. I can remember a programme on TV where several celebrities had it done, and some of the past lives were quite pleasant whilst others were upsetting. I've put Molly and Little Horse to rest now, never to be spoken about again thank goodness, and I look forward to the rest of this life I am fortunately living. I had quite a bumpy ride until I was in my fifties, but I wouldn't change a thing if I could live it all again, because it has made me the person I am today and I'm happy with who I am.

Chapter 9

Those of you who read my first book 'Smiling Angels' will already know what a special relationship I have with my grandson Robert, and I'm delighted that he lives not far away now, after moving from Nottinghamshire. When he was fifteen, like a lot of teenagers he wanted blonde highlights in his hair, so my daughter Tracy would do it for him whenever he wanted her to. It was whilst she was doing his hair one day that she noticed a mole on the top of his head, so off she went to their doctor for him to have a look. The doctor reassured them that it was nothing to worry about, but when Tracy came to do Roberts hair again a few months later, the mole had changed and was a little larger, so off they went to see the doctor again, only to be told once more that there was nothing to worry about. This happened several times in the course of a year with Tracy insisting that Robert be checked over at the local hospital not once but twice, and still they were told there was nothing to worry about. When Robert was sixteen he left school and was looking forward to moving to Cornwall and starting a new life with his mum and step-dad. They moved into a farm cottage at Trerulefoot not far away from us, and Robert started looking for a job and was looking forward to meeting new friends as he didn't know anyone his own age having just moved. The cottage was very old and pretty, and which ever window you looked out of you could see fields and cows. The garden was huge and they set about making it look nice, whilst Tracy made it look homely inside. James and I used to love visiting on a Monday evening and whilst the men played pool in the spare bedroom, Tracy and I either went a walk in the fields or watched the soaps on television. I was thrilled to have all my family close by, and they all loved living at the farm.

They all decided to register with the local doctors surgery after a few weeks, and Tracy mentioned Roberts mole to their new doctor. The doctor carried out a minor operation to take a sample of the mole, and when the results came through, quick as a flash they were told to go to Derriford Hospital in Plymouth to see a specialist urgently about the mole, and once there Robert was given an urgent appointment at the Royal Devon and Exeter Hospital, where he was told the mole was a malignant Melanoma. As he had had the mole for about a year, they operated on Robert very quickly, and he had his head opened up in all directions. I think it was sixty-four stitches and clips he ended up with, and we were all very sad to see Robert in hospital, even though he tried his best to put on a brave face, although underneath he must have been petrified. A few weeks later, Robert had to have another operation to take some of his glands out of his neck but this time, instead of being in a side ward on his own, he was put in a ward with a couple of old men and one aged about fifty. The old man next to Robert had nose cancer and looked in a terrible mess, the one opposite him looked in a very bad way and was always asleep when we visited, and the man in his fifties in the other bed was tall and slim and I remember him having loads of bottles of vitamins on his bedside table. Robert said that he was a health freak, and it was quite amusing in a sad way that the man would put his dressing gown on and go off for a fag outside. Robert was very low by this time and couldn't wait to get out of hospital, and although he didn't say much, just the look in his eyes was enough to see how frightened he really was. He had already gone through a lot, and when he got home he didn't go out much because he had bandages on his head and was embarrassed. When the bandages came off, there was a large patch at the back of his head that had no hair, and Robert was told that it would stay like that unless he had yet another operation later on which would make his hair look alright.

Robert spent the first year of his new life in Cornwall mainly staying indoors and had not been out anywhere to make new friends. He was so busy having hospital or doctors appointments that it just seemed to be his life for a while. After the first year at the farm, they decided to move near to Polperro just four miles away from us, and Robert started to mix with lots of teenagers and make new friends at last. Now nineteen, Robert has had the operation to make his hair alright, and thanks to his surgeon, who is also an excellent plastic surgeon, he looks as good as new. He still has to have a check up at Exeter hospital every three months and a full body scan every year until his five year treatment is finished, and fingers crossed he will be able to get on with the rest of his life. Although he has lots of mates now, Robert spends most of his time with his beautiful girlfriend, and they often come round for a meal. She is a lovely girl and a joy to have around. Robert is always laughing and smiling, and I'm so pleased to see him looking so well and happy. Moving to Cornwall saved his life and I'm sure his angels had a lot to do with it, although I can hear him now thinking what a load of rubbish.

We have all been impressed with the doctors in Cornwall, and nothing is too much trouble for them as they are truly dedicated to their work, so we think ourselves lucky to be living here, and of course it's a wonderful place to live too. Robert did go to a solicitor to see if he had a case for compensation against the hospital doctor in Nottinghamshire who told him there was nothing to worry about with the mole on his head, but thanks to that doctor telling not one but three blatant lies, the case has now collapsed, so apparently pain and loss of earnings don't even come into it. I'd love to meet the doctor in question some day to give him a piece of my mind or even a bloody good slap, but he has to live with it himself at the end of the day, so we'll just have to leave it at that.

Life is still good here in Looe, I continue to work at Looe Gift Shop at the weekends, and it's great to meet the people who buy my books as I get the chance when I'm not too busy to have a chat with them. I often give my address to people who buy my book from the shop if I feel a connection with them, and I save all the letters that I receive as they are all very special to me. I feel truly blessed with my life here in Looe, so it's all thanks to my Smiling Angels who brought me here after my near death experience in Plymouth in 1998. I read a book last year called 'The Secret' by Rhonda Byrne and it was very uplifting. The one thing that stuck in my mind after reading it was the bit about gratitude, and I feel great after practising what is written in the book. I just sit on the garden, in my bedroom or even practise it on a car or bus journey, and start saying "Thank you" for anything I can think of. If I'm looking at the sky, I take a deep breath and under my breath I say thank you for the beautiful sky, birds, trees, flowers, family, pets, the place I live, just anything and whenever niggling thoughts or worries come into my mind, I just block them out with even more thoughts of gratitude. I think the most important thoughts to me are of love, kindness and gratitude. I think thoughts of jealousy are very damaging thoughts to have and bitterness also should be eliminated in whatever way works for you. I have found writing things down helps me to deal with bitterness and asking my angels to help me. Angels only help when you ask them to, so you don't have anything to lose if you try it. I find angels respond in all sorts of different ways to our pleas for help and guidance, and not always straight away, but if you are patient and believe, they will always sort things out for you. THANK YOU ANGELS!

Smiling Angels

By
Suzanne Jennifer Morton

Smiling Angels by Suzanne Jennifer Morton
(Published 2007, Reprinted 2008,
ISBN 978 0 9556020 0 9)

Smiling Angels is recommended by Angelina
Score (Editor, Angels' World Newsletter)

Review Quotes

*The book was easy to read, and I completed it in
just a few hours. However, it lingered in my mind for
considerably longer. To witness the journey from victim
to survivor was uplifting and inspiring.*
    Diane Simms (Broughton Hackett, Worcester)

*Brilliant book, I just couldn't put it down until I'd
finished it.*
    K. Reynolds (East Looe, Cornwall)

A very moving page turner.
        Val Charles (Looe, Cornwall)

We thoroughly enjoyed the book 'Smiling Angels'. What an experience and what a life change! We feel that Suzanne is truly blessed, and that someone in heaven was looking over her and taking good care of her.

Chris and Roger Pulley (Abercynon, Mid-Glamorgan)

Every page was intriguing and compelling reading, written with complete honesty and frankness. I couldn't put the book down, and felt obliged to finish it once I had started. Highly recommended.

H. Leslie (Looe, Cornwall)

This book was so good, I read it twice. A lovely story written by a lady who knows about the ordinary things in life, bringing over the sadness together with the happiness she finds in life and living in Cornwall. It was not too long, and once you pick it up it is compelling reading. Women today are more able to express themselves, and in a lot of cases be self-sufficient. A good read; a follow-up edition would be great!

Ann O'Gorman (Blandford Forum, Dorset)

A fantastic heart warming interpretation of one womans journey of life. Inspiring. Five out of five. Well worth reading.

Ann Griffin (Stoke-on-Trent, Staffs)

Smiling Angels was a book that I couldn't put down until I'd finished it, and one that I will treasure. The bit where Suzanne saw her grandparents moved me, and I feel she was lucky to have encountered such a wonderful experience. I feel fortunate to have met this inspiring lady whilst she was at the gift shop where she works in East Looe, Cornwall.

Lynne Daniels (Kidderminster, Worcestershire)

Wonderful book. I could read it over and over again.

K. Jones (Cornwall)

I really enjoyed it and couldn't put it down. Really lovely.

R. Holloway (Looe, Cornwall)

A very interesting book, inspirational and written from the heart.

C. Greenwood (Cornwall)

A very good read. It is very inspiring to read of one persons battle with illness and the ups and downs that come with it. It made my belief in angels stronger; reading someones experience of being so ill and having her own angels to help her through, and it was great to know there is true love out there for us all together with happy endings.

Lorraine Wakeham (Looe, Cornwall)

I thoroughly enjoyed Smiling Angels and couldn't leave it until I'd finished it.

Muriel Bamford (Ripley, Derbyshire)

You write so beautifully that I feel I know you, and I found your book to be extremely inspiring.

Jill (High Woolaston)

I would like to thank you for sharing your inspiring story, I was really touched by it.

Rebecca (Oxford)

I enjoyed your book (Smiling Angels) it was lovely. I am so looking forward to your next book.

S Sykes (West Yorkshire)

I really couldn't wait to read your book (Smiling Angels) and now I can't wait to hear that you have written another one. What a fasinating story!

Sylvia Baker (Bournemouth, Dorset)

It was a very in depth and touching story, I can relate to why you called your book 'Smiling Angels.'

B Escott (Exeter, Devon)

Your book is fabulous, as soon as I started to read it, I could not stop. Have you written anymore? I would love to read them.

Yahna (Alicante, Spain)

The first thing that drew me to this book was the fact it was a true story. The more I read the book the more I felt that I knew Suzanne, she wrote the book in a way that as you read it you were there with her, not outside looking into her life. I felt that this book took me on a personal journey of my own, giving me inspiration to go out and get what I want from my life, because Suzanne wrote the book in a way that if she can change her life, anyone can.

Karen Fawke (Leamington Spa, Warwickshire)

I really enjoyed it and couldn't put it down, but I did have to keep telling myself that this story is real, as I can't even imagine what real pain and anxiety you went through. Your story is amazing, like a real life fairy tale and good on you to have the courage, you are very inspiring.

D Cohen (Kent)

What an amazing story. I felt moved by your account of the past few years of your life and felt very connected to you. I look forward to your next book and wish you all the best in every way possible.

S Robinson (Plympton, Devon)

Smiling Angels gave me constant goose bumps and has been so inspirational to me. I want to thank you from the bottom of my heart. It was wonderful and I couldn't put it down.

Jacqui (West Midlands)

It's a lovely book, full of inspiration and hope. I am so glad that you eventually found the peace and happiness you deserve.

Karen (Birmingham)

I have just finished your book Smiling Angels and just had to write and let you know how much I loved it and was unable to put it down. Please keep writing your books.

Andrea (Devon)

I found your story so compelling , I couldn't wait to finish it. Your style of writing is very endearing in it's simplicity and I feel like I know you. Your warmth and love of life shines through.

Hazel (Leigh-on-Sea, Essex)

Your book was moving and lovely to read. I am not a reader but I could not put it down.
Sheila (Hastings)

Your book helped me realise that there is a life to live after hard times. The book made me cry and see there is a light at the end of the tunnel, thank you.
Sarita (Alfreton, Derbyshire)